MILES DAVIS
FOR SOLO GUITAR

Arranged by

Jamie Findlay

Cover photo provided by Frank Driggs

ISBN 0-634-02302-0

HAL•LEONARD®
CORPORATION
7777 W. BLUEMOUND RD. P.O. BOX 13819 MILWAUKEE, WI 53213

Visit Hal Leonard Online at
www.halleonard.com

CONTENTS

	Page	CD Track
INTRODUCTION	4	
All Blues	6	1
All of You	15	2
Blue in Green	21	3
Bye Bye Blackbird	25	4
Four	30	5
Freddie Freeloader	34	6
I Could Write a Book	39	7
Milestones	42	8
Nardis	50	9
Nefertiti	57	10
Seven Steps to Heaven	59	11
Solar	67	12
So What	72	13
There Is No Greater Love	79	14
When I Fall in Love	89	15
GUITAR NOTATION LEGEND	92	

INTRODUCTION

When conceiving the idea for this set of manuscripts, I was really concerned with trying to capture some sort of spontaneity that might do justice to and pay homage to Miles' high level of impulsiveness. When listening to Miles, I may hear a fragment of melody laden with arabesques and atmosphere, tone and feel, all surrounded with some sort of magic leaving me with feelings of unity, beauty, light, perfection, and prompting me with the burning question, "How does he do that?" or maybe even more accurately, "How do they do that?" Miles always surrounded himself with the kind of musicians that I'd like to spend much more time investigating, listening to, transcribing, and arranging: Trane, Wayne Shorter, Keith Jarrett, Chick, Jack DeJohnette, Bill Evans, Wynton Kelly, Ron Carter, John Scofield, Cannonball... I suppose the list could go on, but who'd ever want to get to the end?

Trying to narrow down the list of songs was an impossible task, but thankfully the editors helped me there. There are several choices from *Kind of Blue*: "All Blues," "Freddie Freeloader," "Blue in Green," and "So What," a few "must haves" like "Four," "Seven Steps to Heaven," "Milestones," "Solar," "Nefertiti," and "Nardis," and a few of the classic standards we all know from Miles: "All of You," "There is No Greater Love," "Bye Bye Blackbird," "I Could Write a Book," and "When I Fall in Love."

On earlier projects, I would write out the entire set of arrangements and then find myself needing to rewrite a lot of the music because I couldn't keep from veering off the roadmap into improvisation-land. So with this project, I just wrote little notes to myself on a lead sheet, did some reharmonization, and tried to improvise as much as possible on the whole thing. Then I went back and transcribed the rest of it. It was a bit grueling and a lot more work, but I've never felt more satisfied with a book project, and I truly feel fortunate to have the opportunity to share it.

There are techniques used in some of the intros and endings that I love to employ, but may be new for some guitarists: harmonics and open-stringed chords. Luckily, I have a couple of books published with Hal Leonard that will help with that: *Harmonics* and *Creative Chord Concepts.* These books will go a long way in helping to decipher the code of what I'm thinking about when using these techniques.

Almost every song in this collection includes a solo improvisation after I've stated the main melodic theme. I usually try to stay true to the original changes when soloing. Occasionally there might be some reharmonization, but for the most part, the original changes are the ones I follow.

During the entire project, my mother's health had been in decline, and in the last frantic month of transcribing, just after I turned in the last of the work, she passed from this earth. I regret that I didn't get a chance to see and visit her in her final days, and that she was in her final decline while I was pulling notes off the music and writing them down. But it's because of her and my father's encouragement and support all my life that I can even share this music. Almost every time I would need to pay for lessons, get new strings, get a new guitar, or even get a ride to my lesson, week after week, year after year, mom was always, always there. So with that in mind, I humbly dedicate this entire project with utmost gratitude to the memory of Eleanor Sue Moorman Findlay, or as I like to call her, Maw, and just put into these feeble words the enormous feelings of gratitude I have, and say, "Thanks, Maw, I couldn't do it without you."

I sincerely hope you enjoy,

Jamie Findlay

JAMIE FINDLAY

Photo by James Murphy

Jamie Findlay began playing guitar at the age of eight. He has performed almost all types of music: pop, country western, swing, jazz, Brazilian, Latin, folk, and classical, both as a solo performer and in larger ensembles. He's performed with Frank Sinatra, Jr., Dan Seals, Dash Crofts, Russell Ferrante, Alex Acuña, Howard Roberts, Joe Diorio, Ralph Towner, and Red Grammer; has recorded with Buddy Childers, Tierney Sutton, Steve Huffsteter, and his own quartet, the Acoustic Jazz Quartet, among others. He has traveled and performed throughout Europe, Southeast Asia, Brazil, China, Japan, Central America, and in most of the U.S. He is an active music educator, having given guitar workshops all over the world and has contributed to several guitar publications. After several years teaching in the Studio/Jazz Guitar department at USC, Jamie is currently an instructor at Musicians Institute in Hollywood.

Jamie is extremely happy to play a Heritage Sweet 16, a Shoenberg Soloist, and a Ronald Ho Classical. He enthusiastically uses La Bella strings, Seymour Duncan pickups, and the D-Tar Acoustic pre-amp, and loves the sound of his Framus Acoustifier amp.

All Blues

By Miles Davis

*Key signature denotes G Mixolydian.

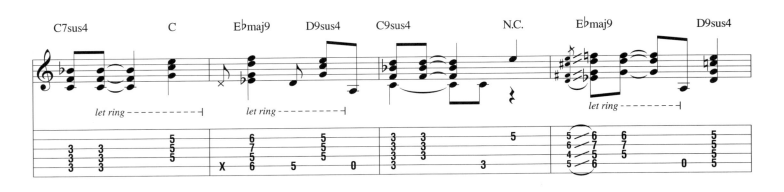

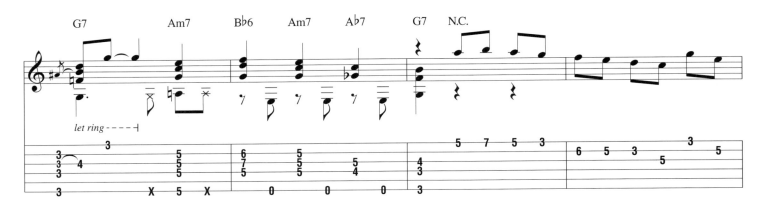

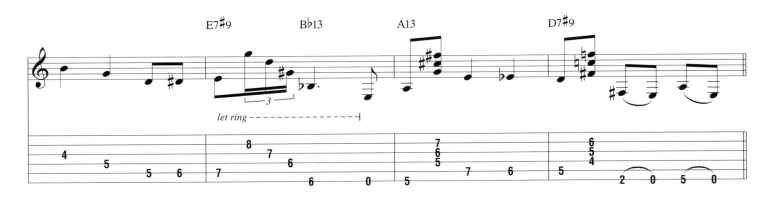

F

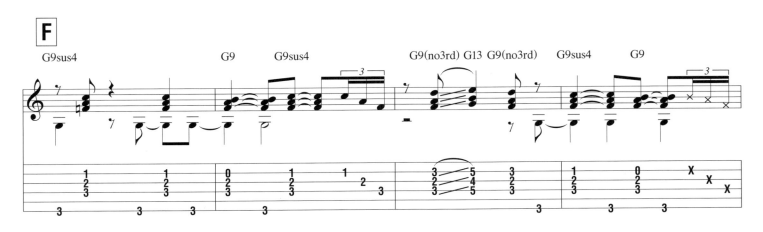

G

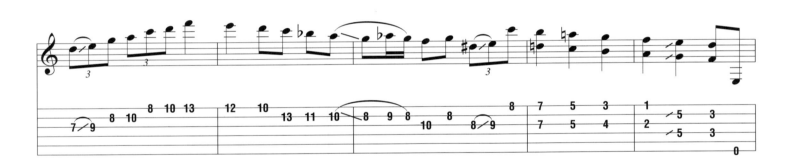

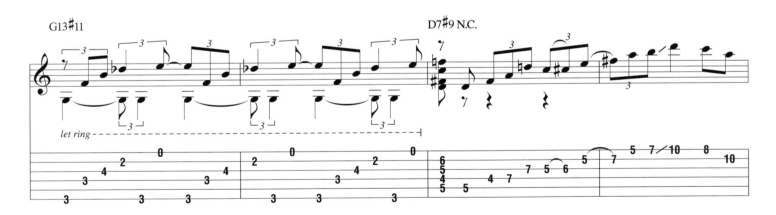

All of You

from SILK STOCKINGS

Words and Music by Cole Porter

Blue in Green

By Miles Davis

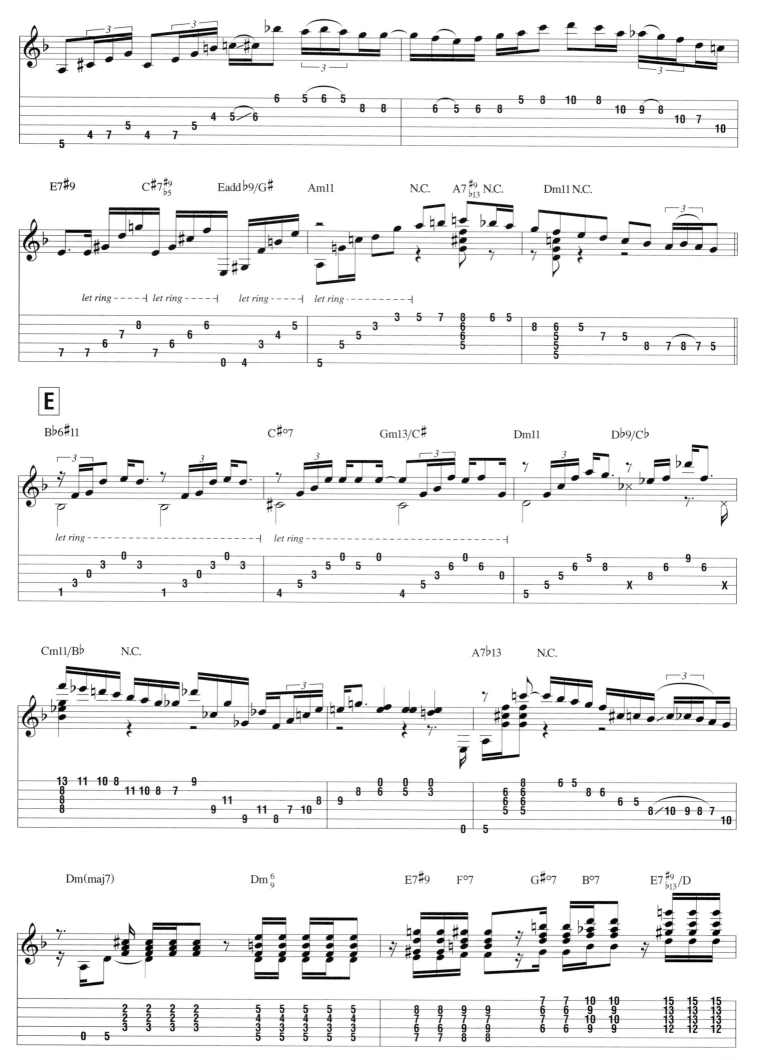

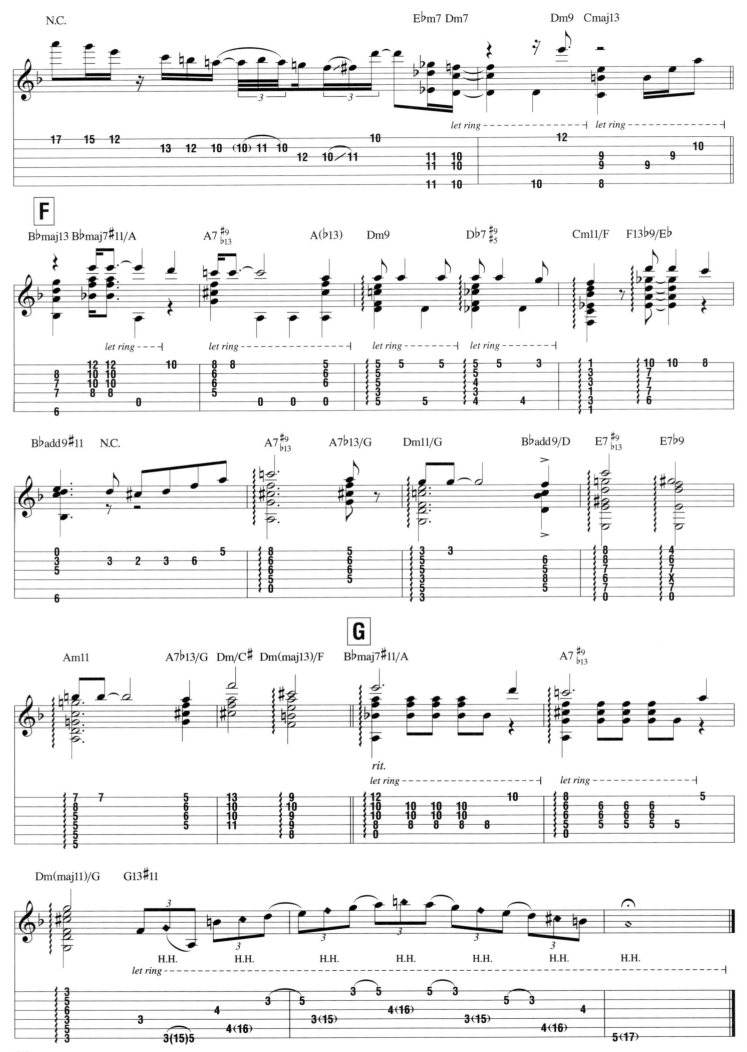

Bye Bye Blackbird

from PETE KELLY'S BLUES

Lyric by Mort Dixon
Music by Ray Henderson

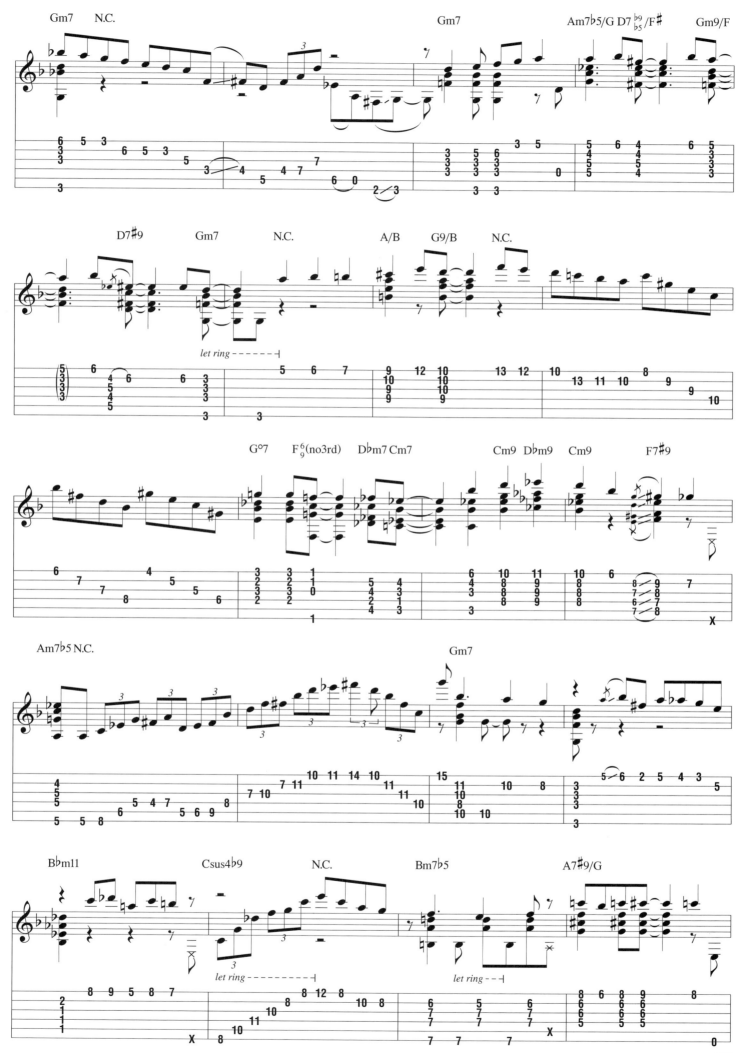

Four

By Miles Davis

*On D.S. add G on 1st string, 3rd fret,
remove F on 4th string, 3rd fret.

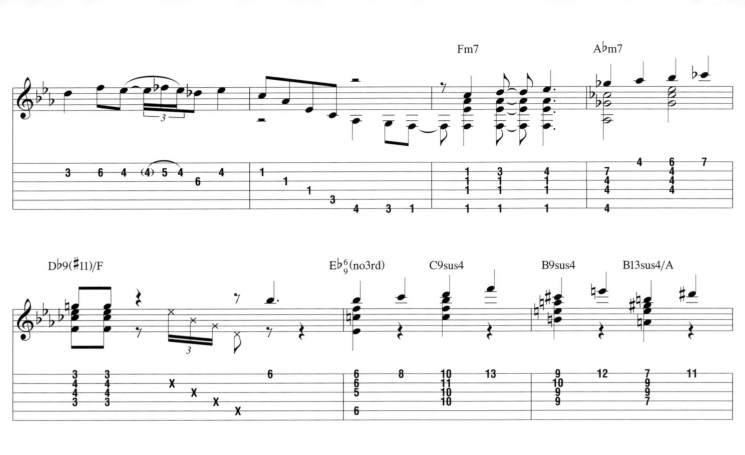

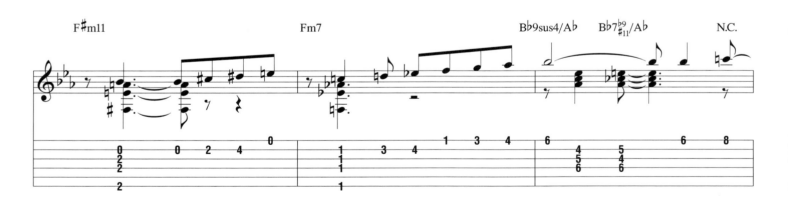

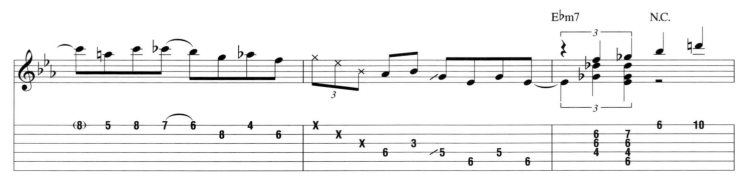

Freddie Freeloader

By Miles Davis

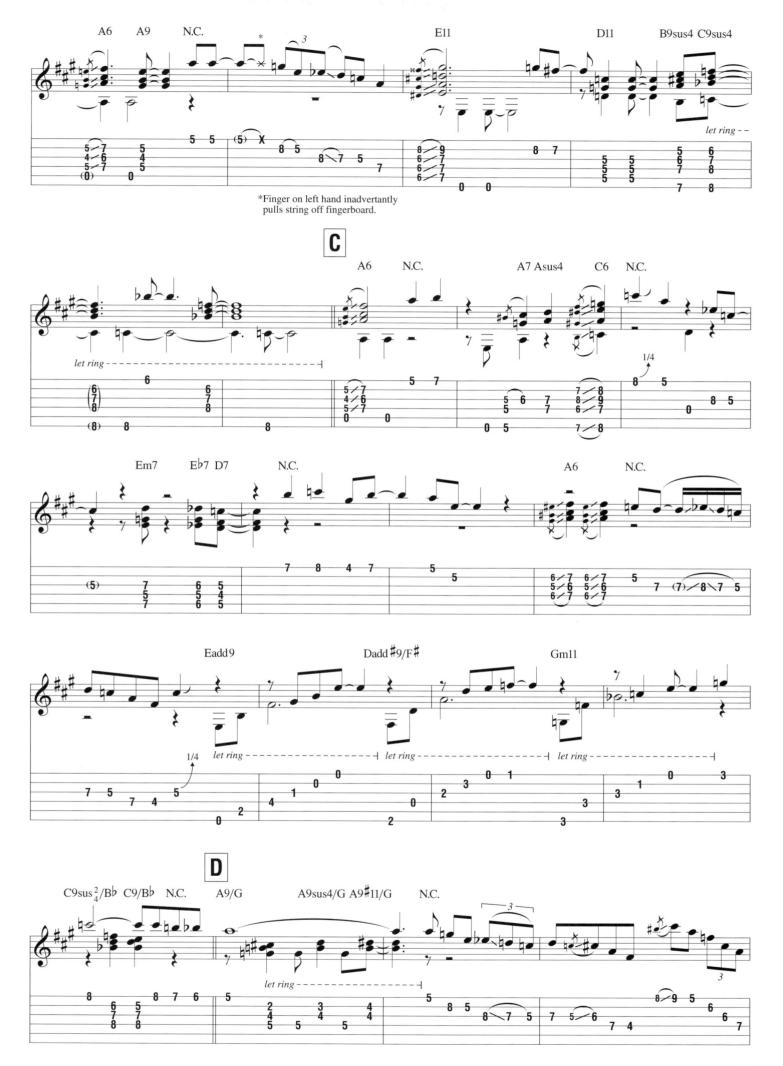

*Finger on left hand inadvertantly
pulls string off fingerboard.

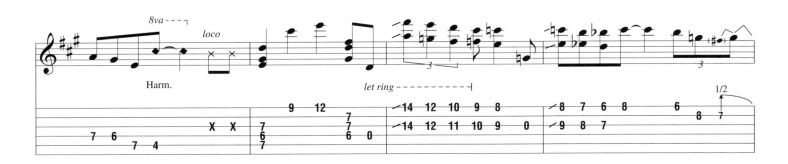

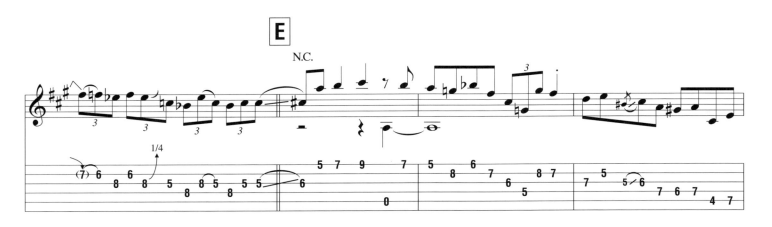

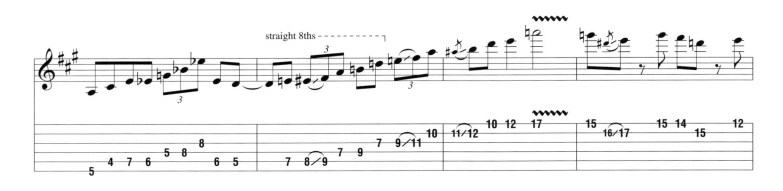

I Could Write a Book

from PAL JOEY

Words by Lorenz Hart
Music by Richard Rodgers

*Angle the first finger to barre from fret 8 on string 1 to fret 9 on string 5.

**Harmonics sounded by R.H. first finger.
(Strum high to low with R.H. third finger.)

Milestones

By Miles Davis

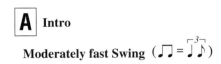

Moderately fast Swing

*Let open D string ring throughout section A.

To Coda ⊕

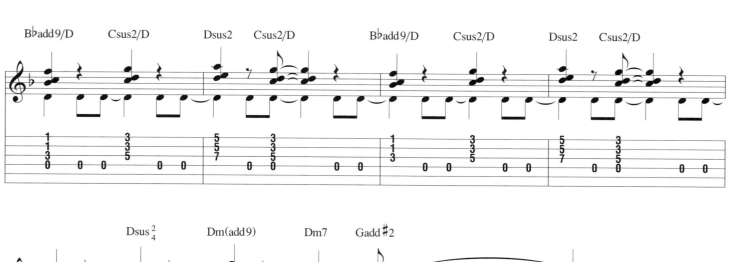

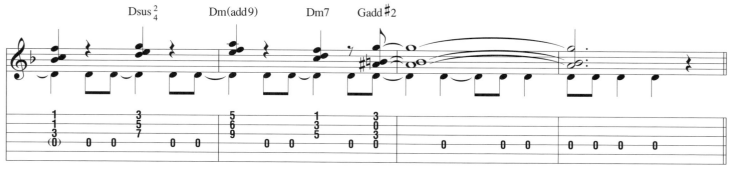

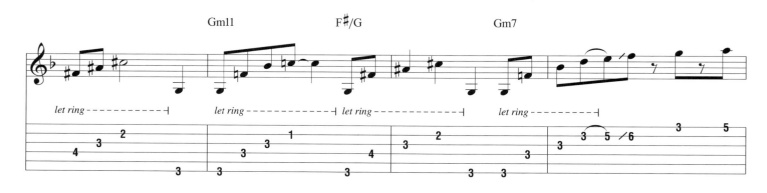

Am7   Gmaj7(no3rd)/A   G$^6_9$/A   Gmaj9(no3rd)/A   G/A   Gmaj9(no3rd)/A   G$^6_9$/A   N.C.

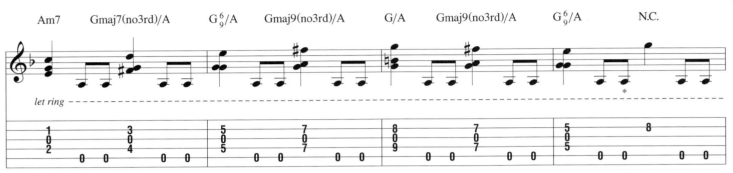

*Let ring applies only to
open 5th string, next
3 meas.

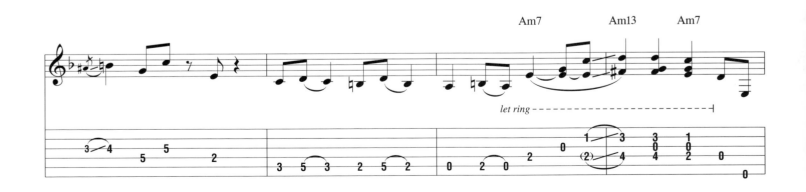

Am7   Am13   Am7

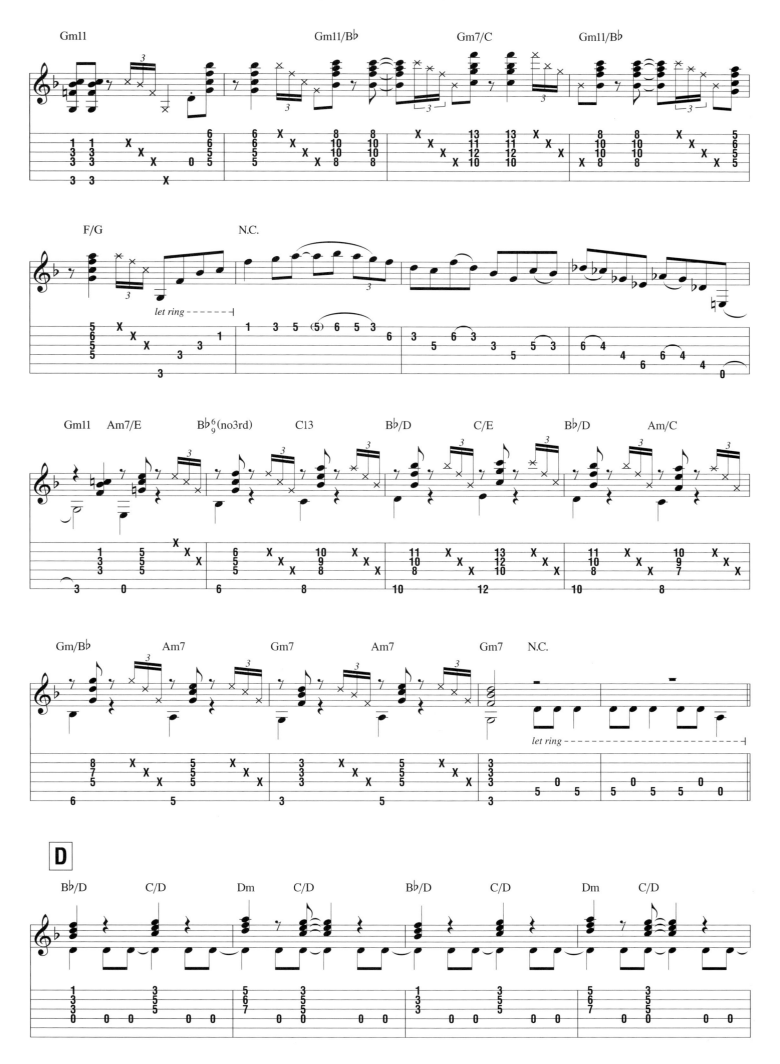

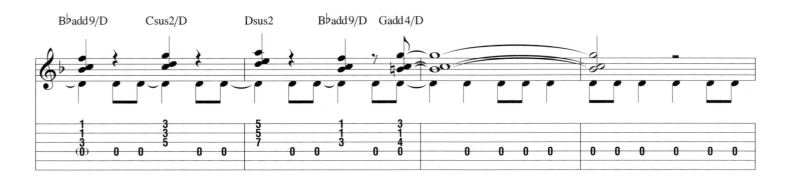

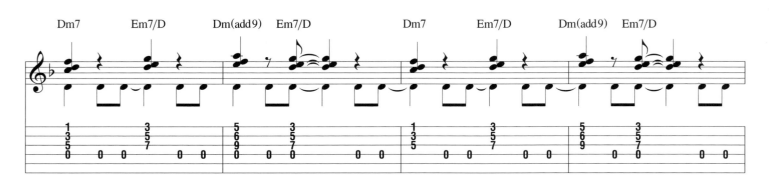

D.S. al Coda

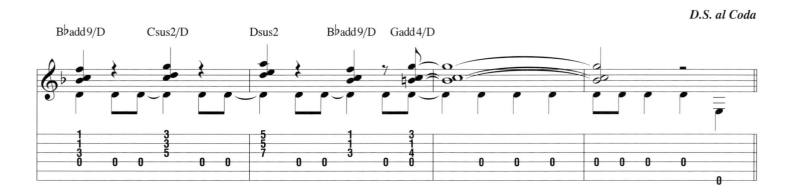

⊕ **Coda**

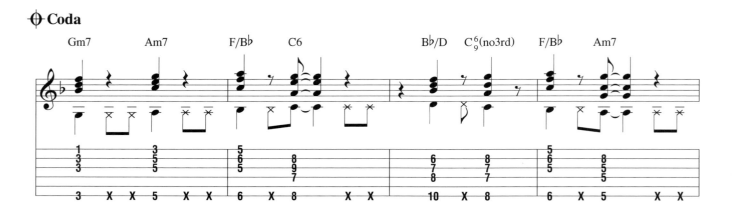

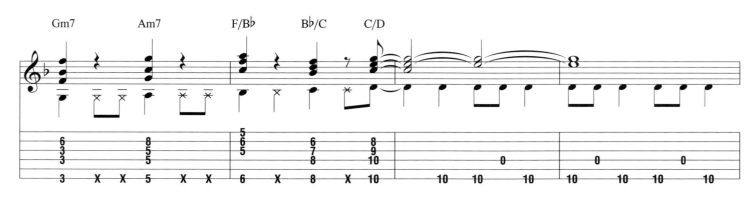

Nardis

By Miles Davis

*Sharply drag R.H. ring
fingernail while strumming
w/ index.

56

Nefertiti

By Wayne Shorter

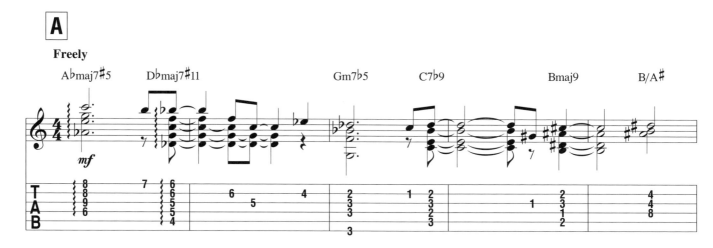

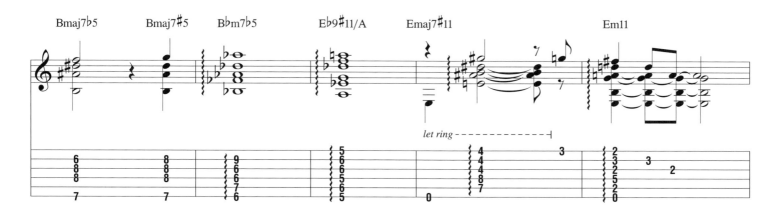

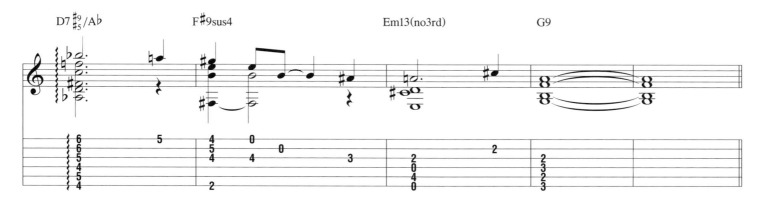

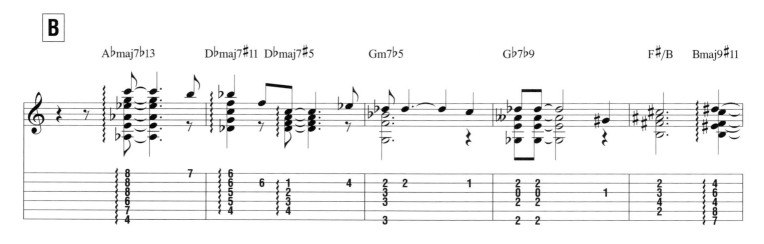

58

Seven Steps to Heaven

By Miles Davis and Victor Feldman

*Muted notes imitate drums.

*Strum behind nut w/ R.H.

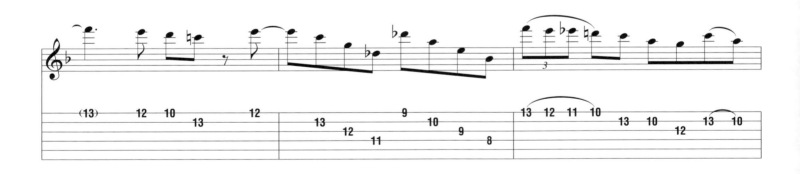

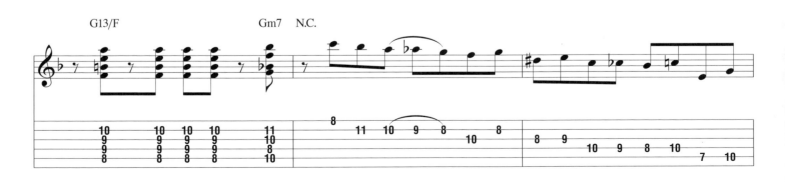

*Strum behind
nut w/ R.H.

Solar

By Miles Davis

So What

By Miles Davis

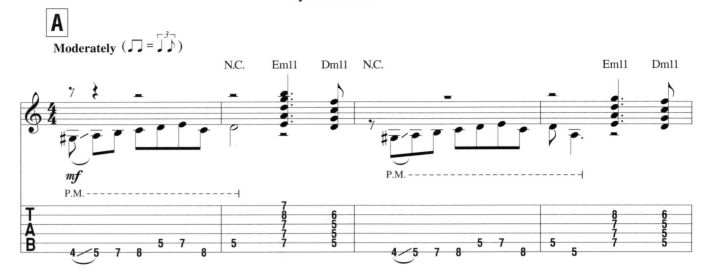

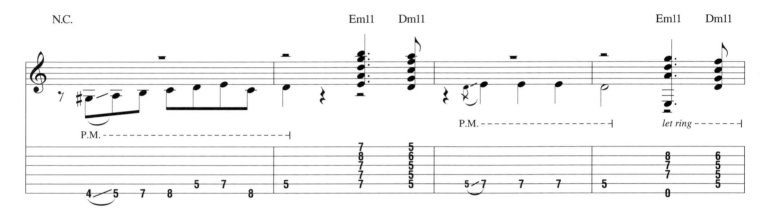

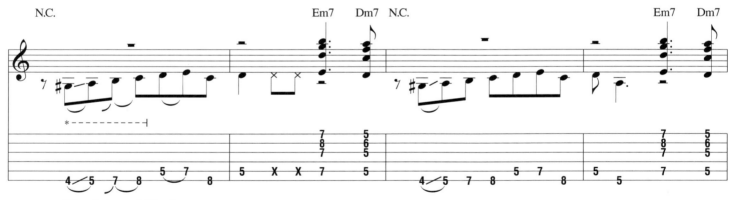

*Played as even eighth notes.

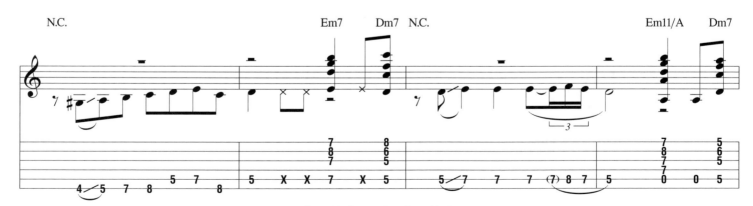

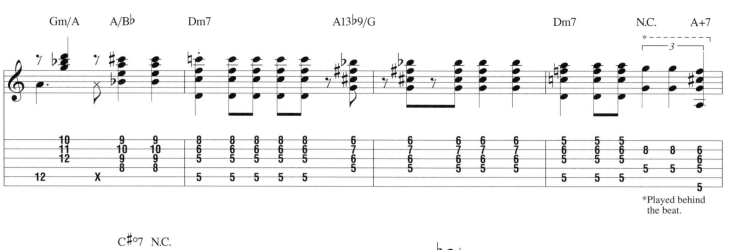

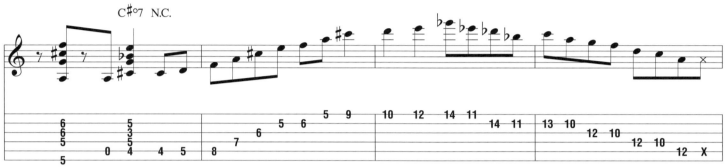

*Played behind
the beat.

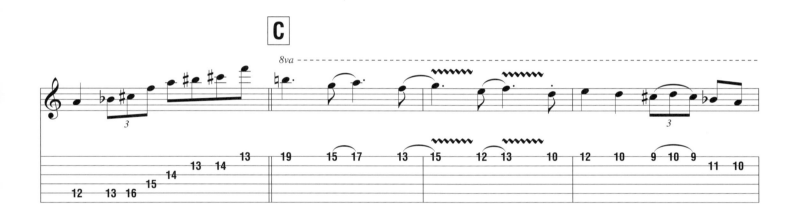

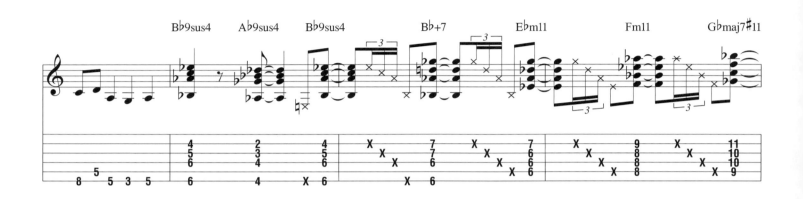

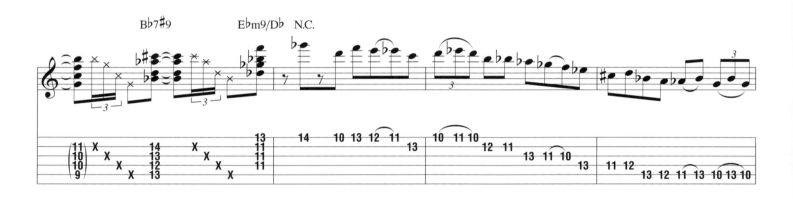

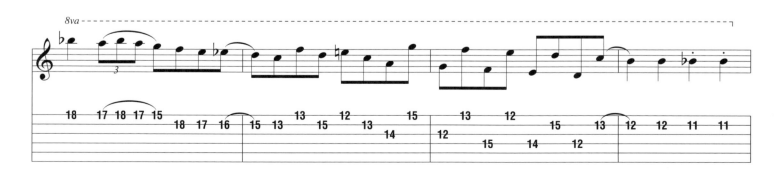

*Rake R.H. ring-fingernail across strings while lightly muting w/ R.H. index finger.

There Is No Greater Love

Words by Marty Symes
Music by Isham Jones

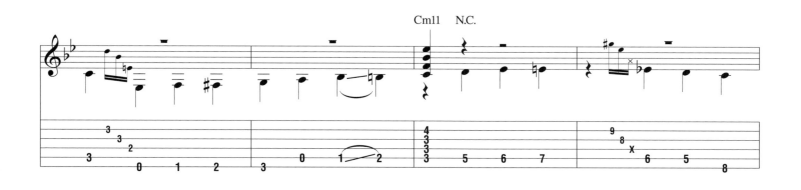

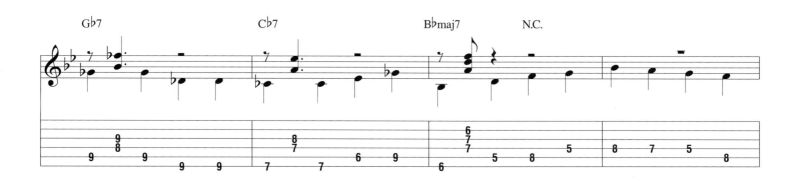

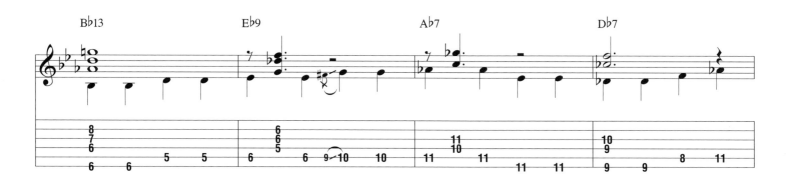

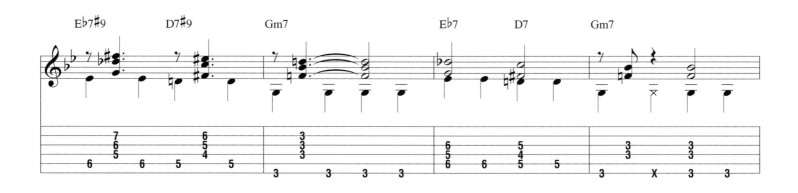

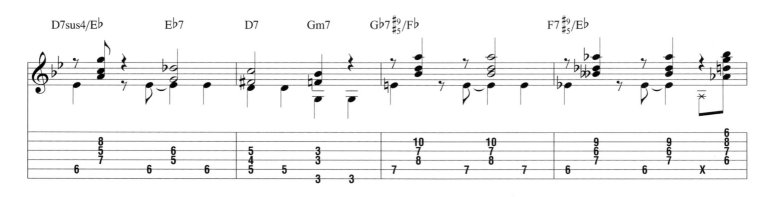

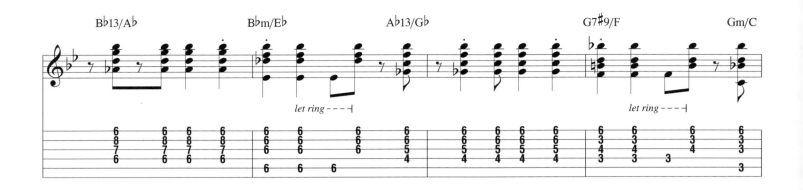

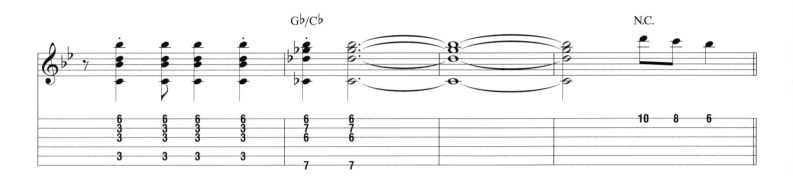

C

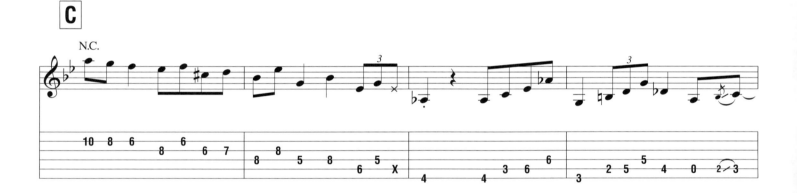

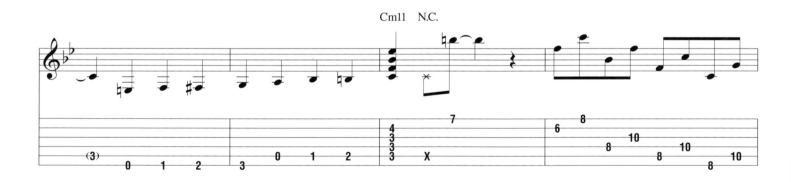

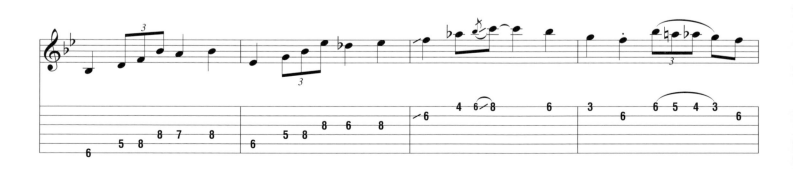

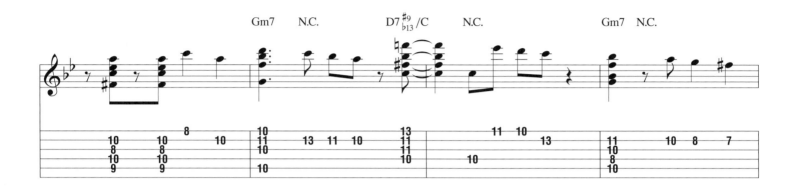

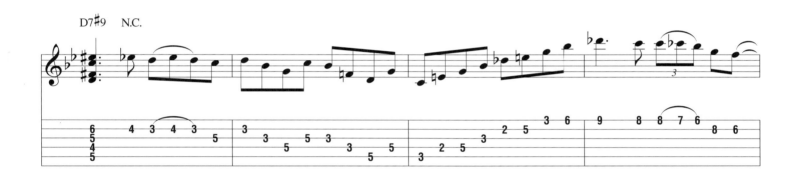

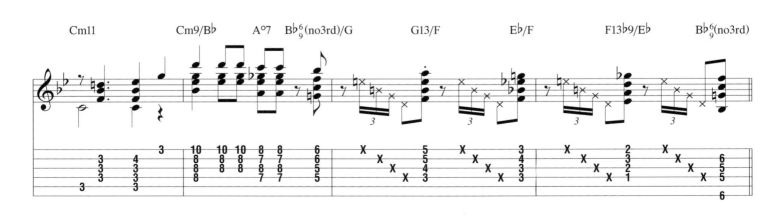

When I Fall in Love

from ONE MINUTE TO ZERO

Words by Edward Heyman
Music by Victor Young

Guitar Notation Legend

Guitar Music can be notated three different ways: on a *musical staff*, in *tablature*, and in *rhythm slashes*.

RHYTHM SLASHES are written above the staff. Strum chords in the rhythm indicated. Use the chord diagrams found at the top of the first page of the transcription for the appropriate chord voicings. Round noteheads indicate single notes.

THE MUSICAL STAFF shows pitches and rhythms and is divided by bar lines into measures. Pitches are named after the first seven letters of the alphabet.

TABLATURE graphically represents the guitar fingerboard. Each horizontal line represents a a string, and each number represents a fret.

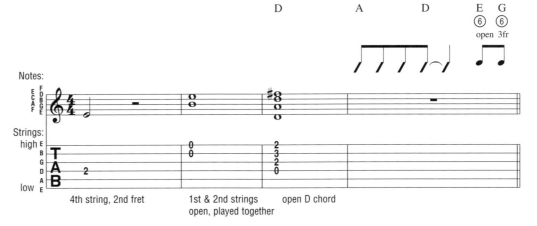

4th string, 2nd fret   1st & 2nd strings open, played together   open D chord

Definitions for Special Guitar Notation

HALF-STEP BEND: Strike the note and bend up 1/2 step.

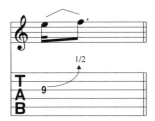

WHOLE-STEP BEND: Strike the note and bend up one step.

GRACE NOTE BEND: Strike the note and immediately bend up as indicated.

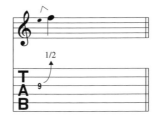

SLIGHT (MICROTONE) BEND: Strike the note and bend up 1/4 step.

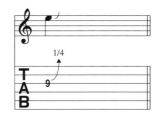

BEND AND RELEASE: Strike the note and bend up as indicated, then release back to the original note. Only the first note is struck.

PRE-BEND: Bend the note as indicated, then strike it.

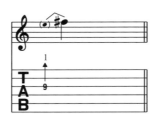

PRE-BEND AND RELEASE: Bend the note as indicated. Strike it and release the bend back to the original note.

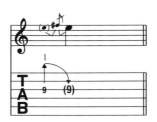

UNISON BEND: Strike the two notes simultaneously and bend the lower note up to the pitch of the higher.

VIBRATO: The string is vibrated by rapidly bending and releasing the note with the fretting hand.

WIDE VIBRATO: The pitch is varied to a greater degree by vibrating with the fretting hand.

HAMMER-ON: Strike the first (lower) note with one finger, then sound the higher note (on the same string) with another finger by fretting it without picking.

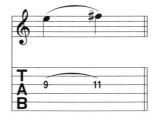

PULL-OFF: Place both fingers on the notes to be sounded. Strike the first note and without picking, pull the finger off to sound the second (lower) note.

LEGATO SLIDE: Strike the first note and then slide the same fret-hand finger up or down to the second note. The second note is not struck.

SHIFT SLIDE: Same as legato slide, except the second note is struck.

TRILL: Very rapidly alternate between the notes indicated by continuously hammering on and pulling off.

TAPPING: Hammer ("tap") the fret indicated with the pick-hand index or middle finger and pull off to the note fretted by the fret hand.

NATURAL HARMONIC: Strike the note while the fret-hand lightly touches the string directly over the fret indicated.

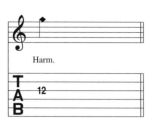

Harm.

PINCH HARMONIC: The note is fretted normally and a harmonic is produced by adding the edge of the thumb or the tip of the index finger of the pick hand to the normal pick attack.

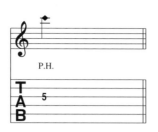

P.H.

HARP HARMONIC: The note is fretted normally and a harmonic is produced by gently resting the pick hand's index finger directly above the indicated fret (in parentheses) while the pick hand's thumb or pick assists by plucking the appropriate string.

H.H.

PICK SCRAPE: The edge of the pick is rubbed down (or up) the string, producing a scratchy sound.

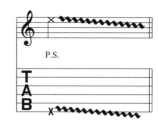

P.S.

MUFFLED STRINGS: A percussive sound is produced by laying the fret hand across the string(s) without depressing, and striking them with the pick hand.

PALM MUTING: The note is partially muted by the pick hand lightly touching the string(s) just before the bridge.

P.M.

RAKE: Drag the pick across the strings indicated with a single motion.

rake - - - -

TREMOLO PICKING: The note is picked as rapidly and continuously as possible.

ARPEGGIATE: Play the notes of the chord indicated by quickly rolling them from bottom to top.

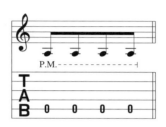

VIBRATO BAR DIVE AND RETURN: The pitch of the note or chord is dropped a specified number of steps (in rhythm) then returned to the original pitch.

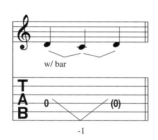

w/ bar

VIBRATO BAR SCOOP: Depress the bar just before striking the note, then quickly release the bar.

w/ bar - - - - - - -

VIBRATO BAR DIP: Strike the note and then immediately drop a specified number of steps, then release back to the original pitch.

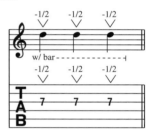

w/ bar - - - - - - - - - -

Additional Musical Definitions

(accent) • Accentuate note (play it louder)

(accent) • Accentuate note with great intensity

(staccato) • Play the note short

• Downstroke

∨ • Upstroke

D.S. al Coda • Go back to the sign (𝄋), then play until the measure marked "*To Coda*," then skip to the section labelled "Coda."

D.C. al Fine • Go back to the beginning of the song and play until the measure marked "*Fine*" (end).

Rhy. Fig. • Label used to recall a recurring accompaniment pattern (usually chordal).

Riff • Label used to recall composed, melodic lines (usually single notes) which recur.

Fill • Label used to identify a brief melodic figure which is to be inserted into the arrangement.

Rhy. Fill • A chordal version of a Fill.

tacet • Instrument is silent (drops out).

• Repeat measures between signs.

‖1. ‖2. • When a repeated section has different endings, play the first ending only the first time and the second ending only the second time.

NOTE: Tablature numbers in parentheses mean:
1. The note is being sustained over a system (note in standard notation is tied), or
2. The note is sustained, but a new articulation (such as a hammer-on, pull-off, slide or vibrato begins), or
3. The note is a barely audible "ghost" note (note in standard notation is also in parentheses).

PLAY THE CLASSICS
JAZZ FOLIOS FOR GUITARISTS

BEST OF JAZZ GUITAR
by Wolf Marshall • Signature Licks

INCLUDES TAB

In this book/CD pack, Wolf Marshall provides a hands-on analysis of 10 of the most frequently played tunes in the jazz genre, as played by the leading guitarists of all time. Features: All the Things You Are • How Insensitive • I'll Remember April • So What • Yesterdays • and more.
00695586 Book/CD Pack..$24.95

50 ESSENTIAL BEBOP HEADS ARRANGED FOR GUITAR

INCLUDES TAB

The best lines of Charlie Parker, Dizzy Gillespie, Thelonious Monk, and many more, for guitar with notes and tab. Includes: Donna Lee • Groovin' High • Ornithology • Confirmation • Epistrophy • and more.
00698990 ....$14.95

GUITAR STANDARDS

Classic Jazz Masters Series

INCLUDES TAB

16 classic jazz guitar performances transcribed note for note with tablature: All of You (Kenny Burrell) • Easter Parade (Herb Ellis) • I'll Remember April (Grant Green) • Lover Man (Django Reinhardt) • Song for My Father (George Benson) • The Way You Look Tonight (Wes Montgomery) • and more. Includes a discography.
00699143 Guitar Transcriptions $14.95

JAZZ BALLADS FOR FINGERSTYLE GUITAR

INCLUDES TAB

21 standards, including: Cry Me a River • Easy to Love • In a Sentimental Mood • Isn't It Romantic? • Mood Indigo • My Funny Valentine • My Romance • Some Enchanted Evening • Stella by Starlight • The Way You Look Tonight • When I Fall in Love • and more.
00699028 Fingerstyle Guitar $12.95

JAZZ CLASSICS FOR SOLO GUITAR

arranged by Robert B. Yelin

INCLUDES TAB

This collection includes excellent chord melody arrangements in standard notation and tablature for 35 all-time jazz favorites: April in Paris • Cry Me a River • Day by Day • God Bless' the Child • It Might as Well Be Spring • Lover • My Romance • Nuages • Satin Doll • Tenderly • Unchained Melody • Wave • and more!
00699279 Solo Guitar $17.95

JAZZ FAVORITES FOR SOLO GUITAR

arranged by Robert B. Yelin

INCLUDES TAB

This fantastic 35-song collection includes lush chord melody arrangements in standard notation and tab: Autumn in New York • Call Me Irresponsible • How Deep Is the Ocean • I Could Write a Book • The Lady Is a Tramp • Mood Indigo • Polka Dots and Moonbeams • Solitude • Take the "A" Train • Where or When • more.
00699278 Solo Guitar $17.95

JAZZ GEMS FOR SOLO GUITAR

arranged by Robert B. Yelin

INCLUDES TAB

35 great solo arrangements of jazz classics, including: After You've Gone • Alice in Wonderland • The Christmas Song • Four • Meditation • Stompin' at the Savoy • Sweet and Lovely • Waltz for Debby • Yardbird Suite • You'll Never Walk Alone • You've Changed • and more.
00699617 Solo Guitar $17.95

JAZZ GUITAR BIBLE

INCLUDES TAB

The one book that has all of the jazz guitar classics transcribed note-for-note, with standard notation and tablature. Includes over 30 songs: Body and Soul • Girl Talk • I'll Remember April • In a Sentimental Mood • My Funny Valentine • Nuages • Satin Doll • So What • Stardust • Take Five • Tangerine • Yardbird Suite • and more.
00690466 Guitar Recorded Versions $19.95

JAZZ GUITAR CHORD MELODIES

arranged & performed by Dan Towey

INCLUDES TAB

This book/CD pack includes complete solo performances of 12 standards, including: All the Things You Are • Body and Soul • My Romance • How Insensitive • My One and Only Love • and more. The arrangements are performance level and range in difficulty from intermediate to advanced.
00698988 Book/CD Pack $19.95

JAZZ GUITAR PLAY-ALONG

Guitar Play-Along Volume 16

INCLUDES TAB

With this book/CD pack, all you have to do is follow the tab, listen to the CD to hear how the guitar should sound, and then play along using the separate backing tracks. 8 songs: All Blues • Bluesette • Footprints • How Insensitive (Insensatez) • Misty • Satin Doll • Stella by Starlight • Tenor Madness.
00699584 Book/CD Pack $12.95

THE JAZZ STANDARDS BOOK

106 fantastic standards in easy guitar format (without tablature). Songs include: Ain't Misbehavin' • Blue Skies • Come Rain or Come Shine • Fly Me to the Moon • Georgia on My Mind • How High the Moon • It Don't Mean a Thing (If It Ain't Got That Swing) • My Romance • Slightly Out of Tune • Tangerine • and more.
00702164 Easy Guitar $15.95

JAZZ STANDARDS FOR FINGERSTYLE GUITAR

INCLUDES TAB

20 songs, including: All the Things You Are • Autumn Leaves • Bluesette • Body and Soul • Fly Me to the Moon • The Girl from Ipanema • How Insensitive • I've Grown Accustomed to Her Face • My Funny Valentine • Satin Doll • Stompin' at the Savoy • and more.
00699029 Fingerstyle Guitar $10.95

JAZZ STANDARDS FOR SOLO GUITAR

arranged by Robert B. Yelin

INCLUDES TAB

35 chord melody guitar arrangements, including: Ain't Misbehavin' • Autumn Leaves • Bewitched • Cherokee • Darn That Dream • Girl Talk • I've Got You Under My Skin • Lullaby of Birdland • My Funny Valentine • A Nightingale Sang in Berkeley Square • Stella by Starlight • The Very Thought of You • and more.
00699277 Solo Guitar $17.95

Prices, contents and availability subject to change without notice.

0805

ARTIST TRANSCRIPTIONS®

Artist Transcriptions are authentic, note-for-note transcriptions of the hottest artists in jazz, pop, and rock today. These outstanding, accurate arrangements are in an easy-to-read format which includes all essential lines. Artist Transcriptions can be used to perform, sequence or reference.

GUITAR & BASS

George Benson
00660113 Guitar Style of $14.95

Pierre Bensusan
00699072 Guitar Book of.................$19.95

Ron Carter
00672331 Acoustic Bass.................$16.95

Stanley Clarke
00672307 The Collection.................$19.95

Al Di Meola
00604041 Cielo E Terra $14.95
00660115 Friday Night in
San Francisco...............$14.95
00604043 Music, Words, Pictures....$14.95

Tal Farlow
00673245 Jazz Style of $19.95

Bela Fleck and the Flecktones
00672359 Melody/Lyrics/Chords......$18.95

Frank Gambale
00672336 Best of $22.95

Jim Hall
00699389 Jazz Guitar Environments ..$19.95
00699306 Exploring Jazz Guitar $17.95

Allan Holdsworth
00604049 Reaching for the
Uncommon Chord $14.95

Leo Kottke
00699215 Eight Songs $14.95

Wes Montgomery
00675536 Guitar Transcriptions $17.95

Joe Pass
00672353 The Collection.................$18.95

John Patitucci
00673216 ....$14.95

Django Reinhardt
00027083 Anthology $14.95
00026711 The Genius of $10.95
00026715 A Treasury of Songs $12.95

Johnny Smith
00672374 Guitar Solos $16.95

Mike Stern
00673224 Guitar Book.....................$16.95

Mark Whitfield
00672320 Guitar Collection.............$19.95

Gary Willis
00672337 The Collection.................$19.95

SAXOPHONE

Julian "Cannonball" Adderley
00673244 The Collection.................$19.95

Michael Brecker
00673237 ....$19.95
00672429 The Collection.................$19.95

The Brecker Brothers
00672351 And All Their Jazz............$19.95
00672447 Best of $19.95

Benny Carter
00672314 The Collection.................$22.95
00672315 Plays Standards $22.95

James Carter
00672394 The Collection.................$19.95

John Coltrane
00672494 A Love Supreme.............$12.95
00672529 Giant Steps.....................$14.95
00672493 Plays Coltrane Changes..$19.95
00672349 Plays Giant Steps $19.95
00672453 Plays Standards $19.95
00673233 Solos................................$22.95

Paul Desmond
00672328 The Collection.................$19.95
00672454 Standard Time $19.95

Kenny Garrett
00672530 The Collection.................$19.95

Stan Getz
00699375 ....$18.95
00672377 Bossa Novas $19.95
00672375 Standards........................$17.95

Coleman Hawkins
00672523 The Collection.................$19.95

Joe Henderson
00672330 Best of $22.95
00673252 Selections from Lush Life
& So Near So Far $19.95

Kenny G
00673239 Best of $19.95
00673229 Breathless.......................$19.95
00672462 Classics in the Key of G ..$19.95
00672485 Faith: A Holiday Album....$14.95
00672373 The Moment $19.95
00672516 Paradise $14.95

Joe Lovano
00672326 The Collection.................$19.95

Jackie McLean
00672498 The Collection.................$19.95

James Moody
00672372 The Collection $19.95

Frank Morgan
00672416 The Collection.................$19.95

Sonny Rollins
00672444 The Collection.................$19.95

David Sanborn
00675000 The Collection.................$16.95

Bud Shank
00672528 The Collection.................$19.95

Wayne Shorter
00672498 New Best of $19.95

Lew Tabackin
00672455 The Collection.................$19.95

Stanley Turrentine
00672334 The Collection.................$19.95

Lester Young
00672524 The Collection.................$19.95

PIANO & KEYBOARD

Monty Alexander
00672338 The Collection.................$19.95
00672487 Plays Standards $19.95

Kenny Barron
00672318 The Collection.................$22.95

Count Basie
00672520 The Collection.................$19.95

Warren Bernhardt
00672364 The Collection.................$19.95

Cyrus Chesnut
00672439 The Collection.................$19.95

Billy Childs
00673242 The Collection.................$19.95

Chick Corea
00672300 Paint the World $12.95

Bill Evans
00672537 At Town Hall $16.95
00672365 The Collection.................$19.95
00672425 Piano Interpretations........$19.95
00672510 Trio, Vol. 1: 1959-1961 ...$24.95
00672511 Trio, Vol. 2: 1962-1965 ...$24.95
00672512 Trio, Vol. 3: 1968-1974 ...$24.95
00672513 Trio, Vol. 4: 1979-1980 ...$24.95

Benny Goodman
00672492 The Collection.................$16.95

Benny Green
00672329 The Collection.................$19.95

Vince Guaraldi
00672486 The Collection.................$19.95

Herbie Hancock
00672419 The Collection.................$19.95

Gene Harris
00672446 The Collection.................$19.95

Hampton Hawes
00672438 The Collection.................$19.95

Ahmad Jamal
00672322 The Collection.................$22.95

CLARINET

Buddy De Franco
00672423 The Collection...............$19.95

FLUTE

Eric Dolphy
00672379 The Collection.................$19.95

James Moody
00672372 The Collection $19.95

James Newton
00660108 Improvising Flute $14.95

Lew Tabackin
00672455 The Collection.................$19.95

TROMBONE

J.J. Johnson
00672332 The Collection.................$19.95

Brad Mehldau
00672476 The Collection.................$19.95

Thelonious Monk
00672388 Best of $19.95
00672389 The Collection.................$19.95
00672390 Jazz Standards, Vol. 1 ....$19.95
00672391 Jazz Standards, Vol. 2 ....$19.95
00672392 Intermediate Piano Solos..$14.95

Jelly Roll Morton
00672433 The Piano Rolls...............$12.95

Oscar Peterson
00672531 Plays Duke Ellington........$19.95
00672534 Very Best of $19.95

Michael Petrucciani
00673226 ....$17.95

Bud Powell
00672371 Classics $19.95
00672376 The Collection.................$19.95

André Previn
00672437 The Collection.................$19.95

Gonzalo Rubalcaba
00672507 The Collection.................$19.95

Horace Silver
00672303 The Collection.................$19.95

Art Tatum
00672316 The Collection.................$22.95
00672355 Solo Book $19.95

Billy Taylor
00672357 The Collection.................$24.95

McCoy Tyner
00673215 ....$16.95

Cedar Walton
00672321 The Collection.................$19.95

Kenny Werner
00672519 The Collection.................$19.95

Teddy Wilson
00672434 The Collection.................$19.95

TRUMPET

Louis Armstrong
00672480 The Collection.................$14.95
00672481 Plays Standards $14.95

Chet Baker
00672435 The Collection.................$19.95

Randy Brecker
00673234 ....$17.95

The Brecker Brothers
00672351 And All Their Jazz............$19.95
00672447 Best of $19.95

Miles Davis
00672448 Originals, Vol. 1 ....$19.95
00672451 Originals, Vol. 2 ....$19.95
00672450 Standards, Vol. 1 ....$19.95
00672449 Standards, Vol. 2 ....$19.95

Dizzy Gillespie
00672479 The Collection.................$19.95

Freddie Hubbard
00673214 ....$14.95

Tom Harrell
00672382 Jazz Trumpet Solos $19.95

Chuck Mangione
00672506 The Collection.................$19.95